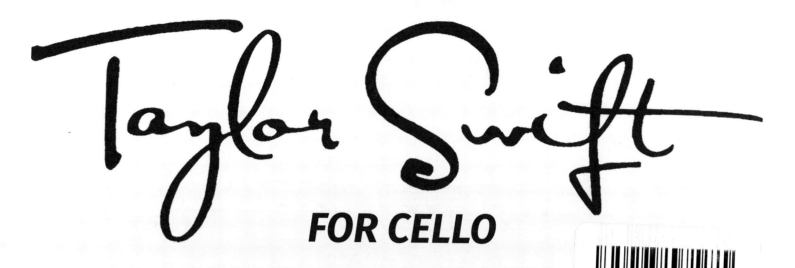

Taylor Swift
FOR CELLO

T0039714

ISBN 978-1-70519-270-2

Visit Hal Leonard Online at
www.halleonard.com

World headquarters, contact:
Hal Leonard
7777 West Bluemound Road
Milwaukee, WI 53213
Email: info@halleonard.com

In Europe, contact:
Hal Leonard Europe Limited
1 Red Place
London, W1K 6PL
Email: info@halleonardeurope.com

In Australia, contact:
Hal Leonard Australia Pty. Ltd.
4 Lentara Court
Cheltenham, Victoria, 3192 Australia
Email: info@halleonard.com.au

ALL TOO WELL

CELLO

Words and Music by TAYLOR SWIFT
and LIZ ROSE

ANTI-HERO

CELLO

Words and Music by TAYLOR SWIFT
and JACK ANTONOFF

CHANGE

CELLO

Words and Music by
TAYLOR SWIFT

BACK TO DECEMBER

CELLO

Words and Music by
TAYLOR SWIFT

D.S. al Coda

CODA

BLANK SPACE

CELLO

Words and Music by TAYLOR SWIFT,
MAX MARTIN and SHELLBACK

Moderately

CARDIGAN

CELLO

Words and Music by TAYLOR SWIFT
and AARON DESSNER

CHAMPAGNE PROBLEMS

Cello

Words and Music by TAYLOR SWIFT
and WILLIAM BOWERY

EVERMORE

CELLO

Words and Music by TAYLOR SWIFT,
WILLIAM BOWERY and JUSTIN VERNON

15

EXILE

Words and Music by TAYLOR SWIFT,
WILLIAM BOWERY and JUSTIN VERNON

CELLO

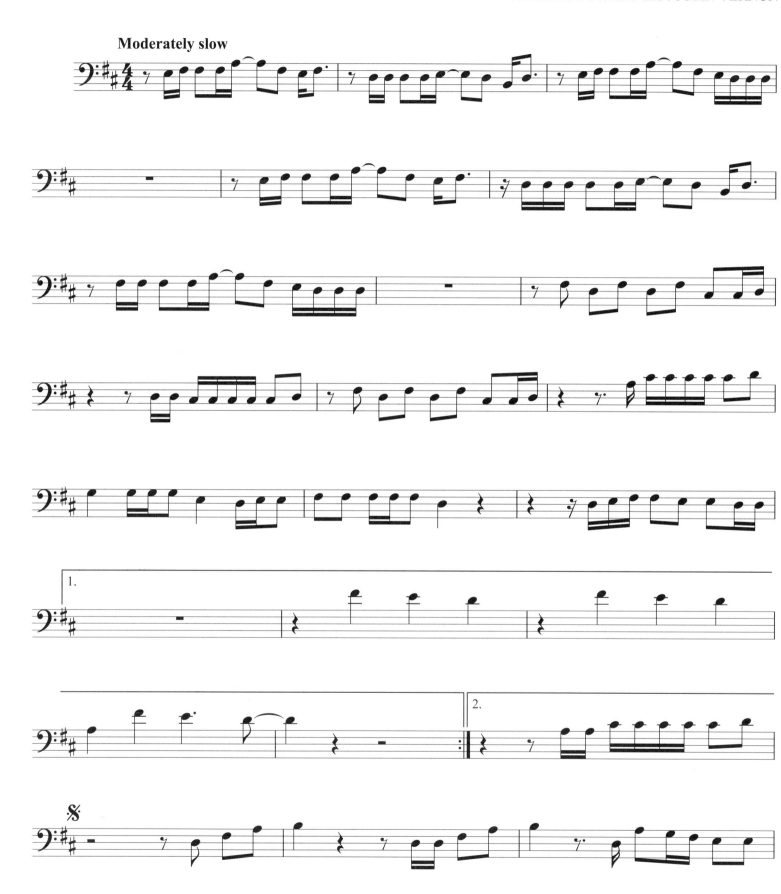

17

FEARLESS

CELLO

Words and Music by TAYLOR SWIFT,
LIZ ROSE and HILLARY LINDSEY

Moderately

FIFTEEN

CELLO

Words and Music by
TAYLOR SWIFT

I KNEW YOU WERE TROUBLE

CELLO

Words and Music by TAYLOR SWIFT,
SHELLBACK and MAX MARTIN

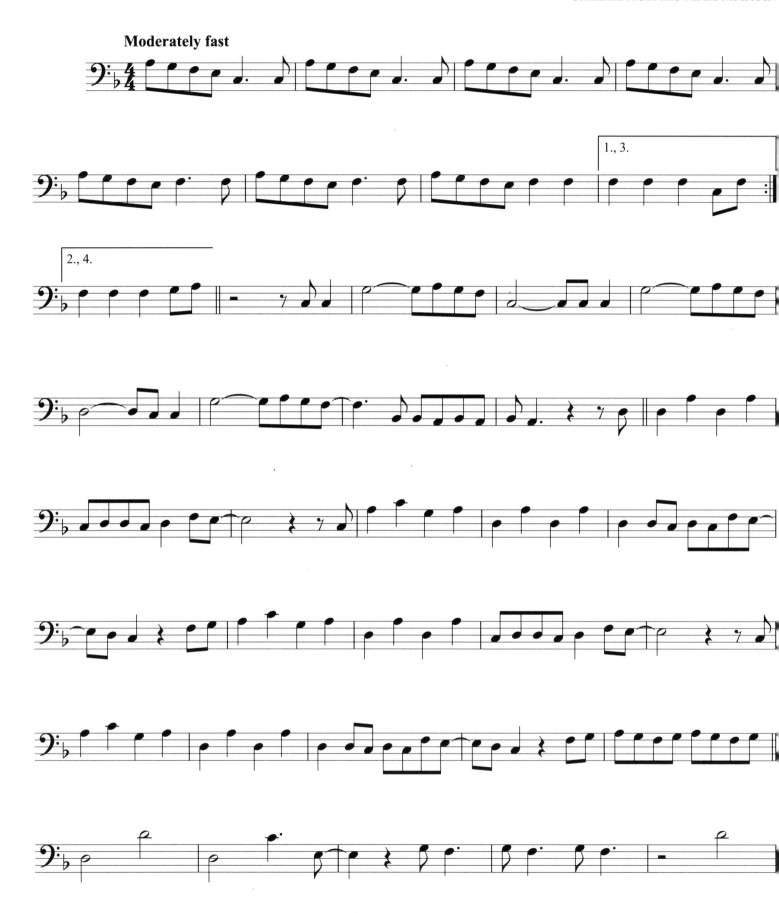

To Coda

D.C. al Coda
(with repeat)

CODA

LAVENDER HAZE

Cello

Words and Music by TAYLOR SWIFT,
ZOË KRAVITZ, JACK ANTONOFF,
MARK ANTHONY SPEARS,
SAM DEW and JAHAAN AKIL SWEET

LOVE STORY

CELLO

Words and Music by
TAYLOR SWIFT

Moderately

MEAN

CELLO

Words and Music by
TAYLOR SWIFT

MINE

CELLO

Words and Music by
TAYLOR SWIFT

Moderately fast

THE 1

CELLO

Words and Music by TAYLOR SWIFT
and AARON DESSNER

D.S. al Coda
(with repeat)

CODA

OUR SONG

CELLO

Words and Music by
TAYLOR SWIFT

35

rit.

PICTURE TO BURN

CELLO

Words and Music by TAYLOR SWIFT
and LIZ ROSE

Moderately

SHAKE IT OFF

CELLO

Words and Music by TAYLOR SWIFT,
MAX MARTIN and SHELLBACK

CODA

SHOULD'VE SAID NO

CELLO

Words and Music by
TAYLOR SWIFT

SPARKS FLY

CELLO

Words and Music by
TAYLOR SWIFT

D.S. al Coda

CODA

SPEAK NOW

CELLO

Words and Music by
TAYLOR SWIFT

SWEET NOTHING

CELLO

Words and Music by TAYLOR SWIFT
and WILLAM BOWERY

D.S. al Coda

CODA

TEARDROPS ON MY GUITAR

CELLO

Words and Music by TAYLOR SWIFT
and LIZ ROSE

49

TODAY WAS A FAIRYTALE

CELLO

Words and Music by
TAYLOR SWIFT

51

D.S. al Coda

CODA

22

CELLO

Words and Music by TAYLOR SWIFT,
SHELLBACK and MAX MARTIN

WE ARE NEVER EVER GETTING BACK TOGETHER

CELLO

Words and Music by TAYLOR SWIFT,
MAX MARTIN and SHELLBACK

WHITE HORSE

CELLO

Words and Music by TAYLOR SWIFT
and LIZ ROSE

Moderately

rit.

WILLOW

CELLO

Words and Music by TAYLOR SWIFT
and AARON DESSNER

D.C. al Coda
(no repeat)

CODA

YOU BELONG WITH ME

CELLO

Words and Music by TAYLOR SWIFT
and LIZ ROSE

YOU NEED TO CALM DOWN

CELLO

Words and Music by TAYLOR SWIFT
and JOEL LITTLE

(small notes optional)

LOOK WHAT YOU MADE ME DO

Cello

Words and Music by TAYLOR SWIFT,
JACK ANTONOFF, RICHARD FAIRBRASS,
FRED FAIRBRASS and ROB MANZOLI